Coffee Houses
of the
Twin Cities

Coffee Houses
of the
Twin Cities

RUTH RASMUSSEN

NODIN PRESS
Minneapolis

Acknowledgments

I am grateful to the following people for their help with the initiation and production of this book:

Carol Orr, who insisted that I write about these coffeehouses "before someone else does!" and then set me up with the perfect liaison. This book would not have happened without her;

Andrea Cohen, the perfect liaison;

And the coffeehouse proprieters who took the time to sit down and talk with me—who made a long journey a little shorter.

Published by
Nodin Press, Inc., a division of Micawber's, Inc.
525 North Third St., Minneapolis, MN 55401
ISBN 0-931714-64-8

1st Printing 1995

Preface

We have become born-again java junkies, baptizing ourselves in coffee. The explosion of coffeehouses around us shows little sign of letting up. There is even a class offered through the University of Minnesota on how to start your own coffee bar.

With the abundance of creative talent in Minneapolis and St. Paul, it's no wonder that our coffeehouses display such innovative style. The Twin Cities coffeehouse experience involves lingering through a cup of freshly ground coffee or an espresso drink while reading, writing, or schmoozing with friends. Games, books and periodicals are often available for our use and sometimes there is live entertainment. Exciting new artwork often decks the walls and recorded music sets the mood. Some of these shops attract streetwise bohemian types, while others call out to resident families. Each coffeehouse has its own distinctive personality.

This book is a compilation of coffeehouses in the Twin Cities Proper, exceptions being made for two suburban bookstores with coffeehouses in them. Establishments which are not, by definition, coffeehouses yet embrace some of the atmosphere are included in a section called Worth Mentioning. Not included in this book are take-out shops which do not encourage an extended stay.

On the following pages you'll find a description of each coffeehouse, including business hours, parking information and smoking designations. With few exceptions, these stores offer espresso drinks, brews of the day, coffee beans by the pound, teas, cold beverages and pastries. Therefore, information that specifies *extended* menu offerings is included instead.

My purpose is purely descriptive; rating the quality of roasting and brewing has been left to you and your fellow coffee connoisseurs.

Undoubtedly, more coffeehouses have opened since this went to press—and more are likely to come. If I've missed any of your favorites or if one has just opened, please write me in care of the publisher so I can add it to future editions.
Viva café!

Table of Contents

MINNEAPOLIS

Downtown Minneapolis

Bar X Espresso   13
Barnes and Noble Café   14
Cafe Metro   15
Café 301   16
Cafe Zev   17
City Lakes Cafe   18
Espresso Royale Caffe   19
Jitters   20
Maravonda   21
Moose & Sadie's   22
The Prairie Star   23

Minneapolis Skyways

Caribou Coffee   24
Starbucks Coffee   25-26
The Daily Grind   27

South Side of Downtown

Coffee Gallery   28
Sebastian Joe's   29
The Laughing Cup   30

Bryn Mawr

Arabica/Bryn Mawr Coffee Shop   31

Northeast Minneapolis

Mighty Fine Deli & Coffeehouse   32

South Minneapolis

A & J Gem Cafe   33
Ashanti Coffee & Bakery   34
Barbara Jo's   35
Blue Moon Coffee Cafe   36
Bob's Java Hut   37
Cafe Wyrd   38
Cafe Tazza   39
Caffetto   40
Calypso Coffee Company   41
Caribou Coffee   42-43
Crema Cafe   44
Cuppa Java   45
Dunn Bros. Coffee   46
Dunn Bros. Coffee   47
Espress Yourself   48
French Meadow Bakery   49
Isles Bun & Coffee Company   50
Java Jack's   51
Java Z   52
Mojo's Espresso Bar and Deli   53
Muddy Waters   54
Napoleon's   55-56
Nokomis Cup   57
Penny University Coffee House   58
Rendezvou Express   59
Sebastian Joe's   60
The Red Sky Grill   61
The Upper Crust   62
Uncommon Grounds   63

University of Minnesota–West Bank

Cafe Etc.   64
Cafe Noir   65
New Riverside Cafe   66
The Hard Times Cafe   67

University of Minnesota–Stadium Village
Croissants & Sweets   68
Espresso Exposé   69

University of Minnesota–Dinkytown
Black Coffee   70
Espresso Royale Caffe   71
Espresso 22   72
The Purple Onion   73

Suburban Book Stores with Coffee Houses
Borders Book Shop and Espresso Bar   74
Caribou Coffee/Book Case   75

Worth Mentioning
Apotheca Natural Juice Bar   76
Bryant Lake Bowl   76
Lucia's Wine Bar   77
Paulina's   77
The Loring Bar & Playhouse   78
The New French Bar   78
Zumbro Cafe   79

ST. PAUL

Downtown St. Paul
Bad Habit Cafe   83
Francesca's Bakery and Cafe   84
Kuppernicus Coffee Gallery   85

West 7th
Babylon Cafe   86

Cathedral Hill
Blair Caffe   87

Crocus Hill
Café con Amoré   88
Caribou Coffee   89
Espresso Extra   90
Rosie's Coffeehouse   91

Midway
Ginkgo Coffeehouse   92
Susan's Coffeehouse & Deli   93

Falcon Heights
The Coffee Grounds   94

University of Minnesota–St. Paul Campus
Lori's Coffee House   95

Macalester-Groveland
A Fine Grind   96
Brewberry's   97
Cuppa Joe   98
Dunn Bros. Coffee   99
Gijo's Coffee Bar   100
Table of Contents   101
Napoleon's   102
Trotter's Country Bakery   103

Highland Park
The Roastery   104
Caribou Coffee   105

Glossary of Terms   107

Minneapolis Coffee Houses

Bar X Espresso

1008 Marquette Avenue
Minneapolis 55402
371-9882

*Smoking section / Sidewalk seating /
Downtown parking*

Monday-Wednesday:
6:00 a.m. - 10:00 p.m.
Thursday-Friday:
6:00 a.m. - 1:00 a.m.
Saturday:
7:00 a.m. - 1:00 a.m.
Sunday:
7:00 a.m.-midnight

Here, across from the new Hilton Hotel, is the right stuff, like gourmet pasta salads, sinful desserts and friendly service. The decor reflects the theater background of one proprietor. The dramatically spackled walls feature two giant pictureless frames (theater props), and at night black lights cast an interesting glow. Goldfish in their individual bowls grace several tables for "cheap therapy." A tongue-in-cheek attitude is epitomized by the credo: "Our mission is to caffeinate the world." Take advantage of the adjoining wine bar.

SPECIALTIES

Sandwiches, soups, pasta salads, bagels

Barnes and Noble Café

Monday-Friday:
7:00 a.m. - 9:30 p.m.
Saturday:
9:30 a.m. - 9:30 p.m.
Sunday:
10:00 a.m. - 7:00 p.m.

801 Nicollet Mall
Minneapolis 55402
371-4443

No smoking / Indoor seating only / Downtown parking

Sandwiched between Midwest Plaza's lobby and the long bookstore counter, this transformation from bank to coffeehouse/ bookstore is a welcome sight. Fresh flowers on each table, complimentary copies of the *Star Tribune* from Barnes & Noble's huge selection of periodicals, stools overlooking the Nicollet Mall and the relaxing atmosphere of a bookstore all make this a desirable stopover. An etching of Stephen King looks down upon quiet patrons, most of whom are reading at the forest green tables and chairs. On "Flavorful Fridays" receive a free shot of Italian syrup in your coffee, and bring your own mug any day and save 10¢ a cup.

SPECIALTIES

Soup and sandwiches

Cafe Metro

108 South Seventh Street
Minneapolis 55402
375-0668

No smoking / Sidewalk seating / Downtown parking

In the Northstar Building off the corner of Marquette and Seventh you'll find an airy, ultramodern jetson-like design, with black tables and chairs, deco lamps hung from the ceiling and walls and tubular lighting slung over the serving area. The large windows provide views of the glassy blue IDS Tower, the Roanoke Building and the hustle and bustle of central downtown.

SPECIALTIES

Light breakfast, sandwiches, salads and baguettes

Café 301

Grain Exchange Building
301 4th Avenue South
Minneapolis 55415
338-5721

No smoking / Sidewalk seating / Street parking

This corner spot, in the North Grain Exchange building, looks out to the original Flour Exchange Building and the old Courthouse. Situated next to its sister cafeteria, these two entities are efficiently run by previous owners of Bonne Viande (Calhoun Square). The huge spinach pie, homemade Stromboli and seven daily coffees make for some great selections. Away from the hustle and bustle of central downtown, its big windows, spacious layout and handsome black & white decor blend to create a soothing atmosphere.

SPECIALTIES
Entrees, sandwiches, soup and salads

Cafe Zev

1362 LaSalle Avenue
Minneapolis 55403
874-8477

Smoking permitted / Patio seating / Parking lot

Monday-Thursday:
6:30 a.m. - 1:00 a.m.
Friday:
6:30 a.m. - 2:00 a.m.
Saturday:
7:30 a.m. - 2:00 a.m.
Sunday:
8:00 a.m. - 1:00 a.m.

When you walk inside the shell of the old car wash you enter another world. This laid back yet lively coffeehouse, with its eclectic chandeliers, changing art exhibits, specially made wooden tables & comfortable chairs brings you back to the days of the early European coffeehouses. A steady flow of customers devote themselves to studying, discussing, playing games from the game table, or just reading in the overstuffed chairs. A baby grand piano waiting to be played sits next to the small stage used for live entertainment in the evening. Check out their light lunch menu, especially the homemade soups and chili. Counter people are relaxed and upbeat and you're made to feel welcome.

SPECIALTIES

Sandwiches, chili, soups and pasta salads

City Lakes Cafe

1200 Nicollet Mall
Minneapolis 55403
371-0688

Monday-Friday:
7:30 a.m. - 3:00 p.m.
Saturday-Sunday:
9:00 a.m. - 2:00 p.m.

Smoking section / Patio seating / Downtown parking

Off the beaten path, this edge-of-downtown cafe quietly provides business people and residents with homestyle lunches and dinners, such as roast beef, lasagna, meat loaf, roast turkey breast and fettucini alfredo. Homemade pies and seasonal treats are on display daily. The nautical decor, focusing on local lakes, includes comfortable, split-level counter seating, uncluttered tables and an authentic patio complete with iron railing and flowering plants. The buoyant atmosphere is devoid of pretense or trendiness.

SPECIALTIES

Hot entrees, sandwiches, salads and chili

Espresso Royale Caffe

1229 Hennepin Avenue
Minneapolis 55403
333-8882

Monday-Friday:
7:00 a.m. - Midnight
Saturday-Sunday:
8:00 a.m. - Midnight

Smoking section / Indoor seating only / Street parking

Located near the Minneapolis Community College, this spacious coffeehouse attracts students, instructors, Laurel Village residents and local employees. The lovely old brick building has huge windows that overlook an upgraded section of Hennepin Avenue. There is no theme or pretense here; just a lot of steady customers studying, reading newspapers and quietly socializing. The counter staff is exceptionally accommodating, which helps explain the tremendous success of this chain, which generally locates near a college or university.

Jitters

1026 Nicollet Mall
Minneapolis 55403
333-8511

Monday-Friday:
6:30 a.m. - Midnight
Saturday-Sunday:
8:00 a.m. - Midnight

Smoking section / Sidewalk seating / Downtown parking

Is it a harem or a 50's era kitchen? You decide. An Arabian nights ceiling, billowy drapes with sashes, some sitting pillows and a black veil over one window suggest a theme, while the vintage formica kitchen tables, one-of-a-kind lamps, and black and white tiled floor suggest another. Brightly painted walls add to the outrageous yet uplifting decor. A side room provides a more intimate living room setting, complete with fish tank. There is live music nightly, and the food is prepared with a low-fat emphasis and looks tempting. Watch for the addition of a wine bar.

SPECIALTIES

Sandwiches, vegetarian chili, soups, salads

Maravonda

430 First Avenue North
Minneapolis 55401
338-7218

Monday-Thursday:
7:30 a.m. - 8:00 p.m.
Friday:
7:30 a.m. - 10:00 p.m.
Saturday:
9:00 a.m. - 10:00 p.m.

Smoking section / Sidewalk seating / Downtown parking

The flavor of Costa Rica and tree branches adorned with strings of lights create an inviting atmosphere in this uniquely designed coffeehouse. Floor-length streetside windows overlook the Loon Cafe, and others look into the Kickernick Building lobby. Help yourself to magazines, books and games on the shelves, and enjoy the soothing music at one of the quaint desklike tables. Café Americano, espresso mixed with hot water, replaces daily brewed coffee, and your first refill is free.

SPECIALTIES

Sandwiches and salads

Moose & Sadie's

212 Third Avenue North
Minneapolis 55401
371-0464

Smoking section / Sidewalk seating /
Street parking

Monday-Thursday:
7:30 a.m. - 11:00 p.m.
Friday:
7:30 a.m. - 2:00 a.m.
Saturday:
9:00 a.m. - 2:00 a.m.
Sunday:
9:00 a.m. - 8:00 p.m

Here is a warehouse-district classic, complete with exposed ducts and pipes, the original hardwood floors, an antique coat-rack, folksy music, Greenpeace flyers and games and periodicals, including back issues of *Rolling Stone Magazine*. Half the walls are rustic brick while the other half is stark white, displaying art. Additional seating has been added around the corner, exposing a creative splash on the back wall. Have a look at the specialty desserts.

SPECIALTIES

Sandwiches, including vegetarian choices, and soup

The Prairie Star

119 North First Street
Minneapolis 55401
341-3526

*No smoking / Sidewalk seating /
Street parking*

Monday-Wednesday:
7:00 a.m. - 11:00 p.m.
Thursday-Friday:
7:00 a.m. - Midnight
Saturday:
8:00 a.m. - Midnight
Sunday:
8:00 a.m. - 10:00 p.m.

A distinct New Age air characterizes this intimate bohemian coffeehouse, with its ceiling stars, tarot cards and a large coffee-table astrology book. Antiquated mismatched furniture and the lavender-painted accents create a colorful and interesting decor. Cozy settings and bookcases brimming with volumes of *National Geographic* encourage reading and quiet conversation.

SPECIALTIES

Soup, "almost always vegetarian",
bread and cheese plates

Caribou Coffee:

Monday-Friday:
6:30 a.m. - 8:00 p.m.
Saturday:
9:00 a.m. - 6:00 p.m.
Sunday:
Noon - 5:00 p.m.

No smoking / Indoor seating only /
Downtown parking /

• Gaviidae Commons
651 Nicollet Mall
338-3814
• Dain Bosworth Plaza (street level)
555 Nicollet Mall
349-9360
• Piper Jaffray Tower
222 South Ninth Street
338-0424
• Rand Tower/First Bank West
527 Marquette Avenue
341-9936

In keeping with their other stores, these skyway Caribou Coffee shops are handsomely designed with the slick modern Euro decor and open-windowed front—all smoke-free. They play sophisticated jazz for the downtown business folks as they sip their power coffees. Some shops provide seating out into the skyway and differ slightly as to hours of operation.

Starbucks Coffee

One Financial Plaza-Skyway Level
120 South Sixth Street
Minneapolis 55402
371-0555

No smoking / Indoor seating only / Downtown parking

Our skyways are becoming home to some fine coffeehouses, the latest being Starbucks Coffee. This is a nationwide chain which originated in Seattle and has several years of experience behind it. Designed for business folks on the run, the high-tech gray counters lining the windows all around provide the only seating; the rest of the floor is for those standing in line. Wall shelves are filled with accessories for brewing as well as assorted novelties with Starbucks' own label: candy-covered beans, cherries and almonds; ground chocolate and vanilla; flavoring syrups; and granola cereal. Starbucks embraces a philosophy: "The proof is in the cup." They are big on quality control and it is evident in the first sip of their coffee. Take note of the special children's menu.

Starbucks Coffee

IDS Skyway
214 Marquette Avenue
Minneapolis 55402
371-0383

Monday-Friday:
6:30 a.m. - 6:30 p.m.
Saturday:
9:00 a.m. - 6:00 p.m.
Sunday:
11:30 a.m. 6:00 p.m.

No smoking / Indoor seating only / Downtown parking

This smaller shop does a tremendous take-away business and provides the same counter seating, sans the windows. Classic Sinatra is in the air and nicely mounted photos of stages of coffee production are on the walls. This is not a place for quiet relaxation, since the hustle of downtown foot traffic abounds here and servers regularly call out drinks as they come up: "Tall latte on the counter!" Condiments surpass cream and sugar; Starbucks offers half & half, whole milk, skim milk, nutmeg, cinnamon, vanilla and chocolate powders, sweet 'n low and raw and refined sugars. Starbucks' own labeled products are for sale here.

Additional Starbucks can be found at:
• **Loring Park**, 1608 Harmon Place, Minneapolis, 673-0804
• **50th & France**, 3939 West 50th Street, Edina, 927-7055
• **Galleria Mall**, 3215 Galleria, Edina, 924-0344
• **Grand & Victoria**, 857 Grand Avenue, St. Paul, 225-0925

The Daily Grind

Commerce at the Crossings
250 Second Avenue South
Minneapolis 55401
339-5886

Monday-Thursday:
6:30 a.m. - 4:00 p.m.
Friday:
6:30 a.m. - 3:30 p.m.
Saturday and Sunday:
Closed

Smoking permitted / Skyway seating / Downtown parking

Although some skyway food shops are designed for take-out traffic, this is a real coffeehouse cafe, complete with rock music, t-shirts for sale and smoke-filled air. A neon sign boasts "world's freshest coffees," and the place is hopping with nearby business folks and highrise residents. The design and atmosphere of this no-nonsense shop is simple and unpretentious.

SPECIALTIES

Soup and pasta salad

Coffee Gallery

715 Franklin Avenue West
Minneapolis 55405
870-9508

Sunday-Thursday:
8:00 a.m. - 11:00 p.m.
Friday-Saturday:
8:00 a.m. - 12:00 p.m.

Smoking section / Sidewalk seating / Street parking

In a bohemian atmosphere with a mixture of used furniture, exposed plumbing, soft bluesy music and eccentric art, patrons read, write, study or play a quiet game of chess amid racks of games, books and alternative journals. As the name suggests, this is an art gallery as well, with a back room that houses artwork and provides more seating. This coffeehouse publishes its own literary magazine, *Java Junkie,* holds open readings and musical performances, mounts a new art exhibit each month and sells jewelry. The food is mostly vegetarian. Among Twin Cities coffeehouses, this one most emulates the beatnik era.

SPECIALTIES

Soups, pasta salads and varieties of Boughatsa
(a Middle Eastern lunch pie)

Sebastian Joe's

1007 Franklin Avenue West

Minneapolis 55405

870-0065

No smoking / Sidewalk seating /
Street parking

Monday-Thursday:
7:00 a.m. - 11:00 p.m.
Friday:
7:00 a.m. - Midnight
Saturday:
8:00 a.m. - Midnight
Sunday:
8:00 a.m. - 11:00 p.m.

Like its sister shop in Linden Hills, this urban Sebastian Joe's has their own line of award-winning ice cream and a savoir faire that keeps it running smoothly. Not of the trendy coffeehouse genre, this shop has been around awhile—and so has its wide customer base. The extra room with its handsome hardwood floor provides an entirely new view with its big east-facing windows. The staff is friendly and the pastries are baked on the premises.

The Laughing Cup

1819 Nicollet Avenue
Minneapolis 55403
870-7015

Monday-Thursday:
6:00 a.m. - Midnight
Friday-Saturday:
6:00 a.m. - 1:00 a.m.
Sunday:
8:00 a.m. - Midnight

Smoking section / Sidewalk seating / Street parking

This unique spot is "home of the brew-ha-ha" and shares a lobby with Stevie Ray's Improv Theatre, although the two businesses are separately owned. The unusual setup gives smokers their own cozy niche, complete with library. Non-smokers can enjoy various settings such as shared seating at the giant wooden table, where there is plenty to read while listening to classical music or jazz.

SPECIALTIES

Sandwiches, soups and salads

Bryn Mawr

Arabica/Bryn Mawr Coffee Shop

230 South Cedar Lake Road
Minneapolis 55405
377-9255

Monday-Friday:
7:00 a.m. - 3:00 p.m.
Saturday-Sunday:
8:30 a.m. - 3:00 p.m.

*Smoking permitted / Sidewalk seating /
Street parking*

Arabica provides Bryn Mawr—and North Minneapolis—with
its sole coffee house, sandwiched between Theodore Wirth
Park and downtown, just north of I-394. This friendly little
neighborhood spot provides a casual and relaxed atmosphere, a
respite from the downtown hustle, with easy access and parking. There is entertainment at the piano on weekends, or you
may happen upon a poetry reading. Expect a tasty lunch here,
since the owner also runs a catering business which provides for
such places as Tazza, Maravonda and Bar X Espresso.

SPECIALTIES

Gourmet sandwiches, soup and salads

Mighty Fine Deli & Coffeehouse

1302 University Avenue Northeast
Minneapolis 55413
331-5851

Monday-Thursday:
7:00 a.m.-9:00 p.m.
Friday:
7:00 a.m.-10:00 p.m.
Saturday:
11:00 a.m.-11:00 p.m.
Closed Sunday

Smoking section / Sidewalk seating / Parking lot

The owner of the Mighty Fine Diner on Second Avenue Northeast opened Northeast Minneapolis' solo coffeehouse just a few blocks east of the diner—and mighty fine it is. The humble exterior will fool you when the interior unfolds into gothic coliseums with second-hand seating and a contemporary counter and stools. There are five daily coffees from which to choose and made-from-scratch baked goods are brought in from the diner. Off this long and spacious room with ample accommodations is the art gallery, a giant room that still feels like the ballet dance studio it once was. Aside from the featured artwork of the month there is a wonderful assortment of items for sale, including magnetic poetry kits, kids tie-dyed denim jackets, artsy cards and posters. This classic corner locale, which is neighbor to The Modern Cafe and the old Ritz Theater, attracts artists, locals and instructors from nearby schools.

SPECIALTIES

Sandwiches, salads, soup, Sebastian Joe's ice cream

South Minneapolis

A & J Gem Cafe

Monday-Sunday:
6:00 a.m. - 2:00 p.m.

2827 Hennepin Avenue South
Minneapolis 55408
874-1225

Smoking section / Indoor seating / Parking lot

Ever since I can remember, this little hole-in-the-wall has served food under one name or another. Since 1978 it has mostly been the Gem Cafe, a classic diner that has quietly served its small but local following as well as many of our local celebs and moviemakers passing through town. Recently they've expanded into a large room which serves as the espresso bar. The new room provides ample seating, pink neon lighting and a "gem" of a neon clock. Walls display a hodgepodge of art as well as daily food specials, and music is from an oldies station to match the '40s decor.

SPECIALTIES
Full breakfast and light lunch

Ashanti Coffee & Bakery

4616 Nicollet Avenue South
Minneapolis 55409

No smoking / Sidewalk seating /
Parking lot

Monday-Friday:
7:00 a.m. - 7:00 p.m.
Saturday:
7:00 a.m. - 6:00 p.m.
Sunday:
8:00 a.m. - 6:00 p.m

In this mini mall, and Sherman Bakery's former spot, is a new bakery and coffeehouse. The simple, non-trendy room holds a handful of high tables and handsome stools. Racks hold both day-old and two-day-old baked goods, as well as unique brands of coffee and espresso from Cuba, Peurto Rico and the Caribbean. Take advantage of the Jamaican/Caribbean influence, from the jerk chicken to the hot spiced lunch patty. Unique beverage offerings include ginger beer, Ting and authentic English teas.

SPECIALTIES

Jamaican/Caribbean specialties, soup, salad, ice cream

Barbara Jo's

4002 Minnehaha Avenue South
Minneapolis 55406
722-7231

No smoking / Sidewalk seating / Street parking

This small shop, with its feminine touch and European look, is tidy and relaxing, with plants in the window and Ricky Lee Jones on the stereo. There is a small set of little marble-topped tables and shelves of local newspapers. A collage of photos and articles reveals the store's history and one prominent phrase explains its philosophy: "Mama wouldn't let you dunk, but we insist." Barbara Jo's homemade biscottis are the house specialty. There is quite a variety of them, and you may sample pieces from the self-serve cookie jar. If you've never tried these Italian dunking bisquits, this would be the place to begin.

SPECIALTIES

Sandwiches and soup

Blue Moon Coffee Cafe

3822 East Lake Street
Minneapolis
721–9230

Sunday-Thursday
7:00 a.m.-9:00 p.m.
Friday-Saturday
7:00 a.m.-11:00 p.m.

No smoking/Sidewalk seating/Street parking

Dark tongue and groove pine floor, lavendar ceiling and ducts, and red chairs make a colorful impression in this nicely arranged room. The nifty bar is supported by circa 1950s glass blocks that also grace the entrance, and colored lighting in them adds to the allure. Sit at one of the spaciously situated lacquered wood tables or step up to the quaint den setting in the back, with upholstered furniture, decks of cards, games and periodicals. The mellow music and patrons are welcoming, as is the sunshine flooding through the southern windows.

Bob's Java Hut

2708 Lyndale Avenue South
Minneapolis 55408
871-4485

*Smoking permitted / Sidewalk seating /
Street parking*

Monday-Thursday:
7:00 a.m. - 11:00 p.m.
Friday:
7:00 a.m. - Midnight
Saturday:
8:00 a.m. - Midnight
Sunday:
8:00 a.m. - 11:00 p.m.

This long room with its rustic wood floor, 50s-era kitchen furniture and alternative rock from the juke box attracts a young crowd and is somewhat reminiscent of Muddy Waters. What gives this coffeehouse its very own flavor is the motorcycle racing motif. There is a giant racing stripe on the ceiling, motorcycle wallhangings and street signs. A large slate counter sits atop milk-box aluminum, from where you may order plain old donuts and Kool-aid. If you happen to have Fido in toe, grab him a complimentary dog biscuit. Fairly quiet by day, this swells into a hot spot at night, adding to the neighborhood's growing cluster of late-night coffeehouses.

Cafe Wyrd

1600 West Lake Street
Minneapolis 55408
827-5710

Smoking section / Sidewalk seating / Street parking

"Wyrd" refers to fate or destiny, as prophesied by the "wierd systers" in Shakespeare's Macbeth. Light floods through the big windows for good reading at this home to students and Uptown local color. During the warm months the east-facing sidewalk seating against the whitewashed wall receives the best morning rays of anywhere in town. Inside seating includes bar stools and a back area for smokers. Games and an array of local publications are gathered up front. At night the rock music is cranked up a bit as the crowd expands into Wyrd's late-night hours. The vegetarian menu features artichoke pâté, a bread and cheese plate and vegetable soups. The pastries are homemade and coffee is served with an imported bisquit.

SPECIALTIES

Soups, salads, fruit plate and appetizers

Cafe Tazza

3001 Hennepin Avenue South
Minneapolis 55408
825-9707

*No smoking / Indoor seating only /
Ramp parking*

Monday-Thursday:
8:00 a.m. - Midnight
Friday:
8:00 a.m. - 1:00 a.m.
Saturday:
9:00 a.m. - 1:00 a.m.
Sunday:
9:00 a.m. - Midnight

The name and ambience are Italian (pronounced "totsa") and avant-garde, with coliseum-like archways, rich counter stonework, giant pictureless frames and Victorian wallpaper hung in a most unusual manner. Tazza's greatest draw may be its terrace, a premier people-watching spot outside the shop but inside Calhoun Square, across from Figlios. Besides the coffee, there's a changing variety of wines and imported beer. By night this place is effervescent, overflowing with couples who enjoy the romantic candlelight inside and others who just enjoy being where it's at. Or maybe they come for the desserts . . .

SPECIALTIES
Sandwiches, daily soup and pasta salads

Caffetto

708 West 22nd Street
Minneapolis 55405
872-0911

Sunday-Thursday:
8:00 a.m. - 11:00 p.m.
Friday-Saturday:
8:00 a.m. - Midnight

Smoking section / Sidewalk seating / Street parking

Heavy on the bohemian side, this decor almost rivals the Loring Bar: funky mixture of furniture, bar seating, a single vinyl booth, and an old bottled Coke dispenser. Offbeat music and the select crowd of regulars add to the eccentric image. Coffee is served in assorted kitchen-friendly mugs.

SPECIALTIES

Spinach pie, Turkish salad, hummus, gyros, baklava
and shakes

Calypso Coffee Company

3238 West Lake Street
Minneapolis 55416
929-5799

Sunday-Thursday:
7:00 a.m. - 10:00 p.m.
Friday & Saturday:
7:00 a.m. - 11:00 p.m.

No smoking / Sidewalk seating / Parking lot

This "coffee and yogurt bar" serves some excellent frozen yogurt in addition to its daily coffees. The tropical decor is bright and light, with turquoise and purple accents, large plants, and Greek-white walls. The ample seating includes window bars overlooking Calhoun Village and, if you look hard enough, Lake Calhoun. If that doesn't interest you, turn your gaze to the 3-D wall posters that are all the rage and are also for sale. Don't miss the desserts like chocolate killer cake.

SPECIALTIES

Sandwiches, including vegetarian, bagels and pasta salads

Caribou Coffee

2922 Hennepin Avenue South
Minneapolis 55408
824-2025

No smoking / Sidewalk seating / Street parking

Monday-Thursday:
7:00 a.m. - 10:00 p.m.
Friday:
7:00 a.m. - 11:00 p.m.
Saturday:
8:00 a.m. - 11:00 p.m.
Sunday:
8:00 a.m. - 10:00 p.m

This store, part of a chain of several, displays a unique "daily ritual" ceiling and two walls of French windows, usually open in the warm months. This spot provides a good view of the Lake and Hennepin corner—possibly the best people-watching in town. The mostly take-out business and quiet morning lingerers are replaced at night by families and couples crowding in, especially for the Saturday night musical entertainment. The gourmet desserts are always tempting here.

Caribou Coffee

4408 France Avenue South
Edina 55410
926-7086

No smoking / Sidewalk seating / Parking lot

Sunday-Thursday:
6:30 a.m. - 10:00 p.m.
Friday-Saturday:
6:30 a.m. - 11:00 p.m.

This small shop has a door into a larger Bruegger's Bagels as does its shop in Highland Park. The design is modern Scandinavian as in the other Caribou stores, and its staff is exceptionally friendly and patient. The chain of stores specializes in a wide variety of gourmet desserts. This Caribou tends to attract more of a family crowd because of its residential neighborhood and quaint corner locale near a hardware store and barber shop.

Caribou Coffee

815 West 50th Street

Minneapolis 55409

825-8255

Sunday-Thursday:
6:30 a.m. - 10:00 p.m.
Friday-Saturday:
6:30 a.m. - 11:00 p.m.

No smoking / Indoor seating only / Parking lot

This store is a bit more spacious than some of Caribou's smaller shops, and is situated between a bookstore and a deli, near The Malt Shop. Its decor includes a subdued cream color, sleek polished wood-framed windows, bar seating and a curved room that wraps around the arched counter. Off the end of the bar is a selection of their novelty gifts, including a nifty tile plaque of Caribou's moose logo. All Caribou Coffees carry pastries from Goodfellow's four-star restaurant.

Crema Cafe

3403 Lyndale Avenue South
Minneapolis 55408
824-3868

*No smoking /
Sidewalk seating /
Street parking*

Monday-Friday:
6:30 a.m.–11:00 p.m.
Saturday:
7:00 a.m. - 11:00 p.m.
Sunday:
9:00 a.m. - 8:00 p.m.
Winter hours
Monday-Friday:
6:30 a.m. - 9:00 p.m.
Saturday:
7:00 a.m. - 9:00 p.m.
Sunday:
9:00 a.m. - 6:00 p.m.

Crema's decor is enchanting, from the gothic old-world walls and stained-glass windows to the water fountain and partly cloudy ceiling. The chic ice cream cases came by boat from Italy, which is where the coffee beans are roasted. Next door is where Sonny's Ice Cream is made, and Crema takes full advantage of their top-notch product by serving it up in flavors like kahlua fudge brownie, pistachio and spumoni. A variety of musical and literary entertainment is performed weekly on a small stage.

SPECIALTIES

Specialty sandwiches and gourmet ice cream

Cuppa Java

3940 West 50th Street

Edina 55410

928-9004

No smoking / Indoor seating only / Parking lot

Monday-Wednesday:
6:30 a.m. - 6:00 p.m.
Thursday:
6:30 a.m. - 8:00 p.m.
Friday-Saturday:
6:30 a.m. - 6:00 p.m.
Sunday:
10:00 a.m. - 5:00 p.m.

This small shop has a surprise upper level loft that overlooks a cobblestone walkway—like a little watchtower. Both levels have windows all around for a bright environment. This cute spot is hidden from all but the local passersby in its location behind the 5-0 Mall. Not enough people take advantage of the upper level seating; most patrons are the local business folks breezing in and out for a to-go cup or sandwich. Coffee is self-serve with free refills.

SPECIALTIES

Sandwiches, bagels and salads.

Dunn Bros. Coffee

1506 West Lake Street
Minneapolis 55408
827-5094

No smoking / Patio seating / Parking lot

During the colder months this small shop fills mostly take-out orders, since the seating is very limited. For the rest of the year the front patio shares space with Bruegger's Bagels and Pop's candy and popcorn shop. Dunn Bros. Coffee has slowly grown to a chain of four, including its location across from Ridgedale, where it also shares space with Brueggers Bagels. With a roaster on the premises and educational displays providing advice and coffee terminology, these shops are almost little coffee museums, complete with gift shops.

Dunn Bros. Coffee

3348 Hennepin Avenue South
Minneapolis 55408
822-3292

Sunday-Thursday:
7:00 a.m. - 10:00 p.m.
Friday-Saturday:
7:00 a.m. - 11:00 p.m.

No smoking / Sidewalk seating / Parking lot

Set into a residential neighborhood just blocks from the Lake & Hennepin commotion, this completely renovated double lot houses the newest Dunn Bros. Coffee—a spacious departure from its smaller shops. More closely resembling its St. Paul store, there are two large rooms with giant front windows facing Hennepin Avenue. The shiny new roaster, a Dunn Bros staple, takes precedence in the main room and allows for a handful of tables. There is more seating in the next room, as well as photographic art from Dunn Bros favorite artist. Walls have been painted a soothing off-white and the renovation has retained the flavor of Uptown and the original structure with its tin ceiling, old radiators and painted floorboards. Black tiled floors match the black tables, and teal accents the chairs. Wood benches and track lighting complete the handsome decor.

Espress Yourself

5445 - 28th Avenue South

Minneapolis 55417

729-1505

Monday-Thursday:
7:00 a.m. - 10:00 p.m.
Friday-Saturday:
9:00 a.m. - 9:00 p.m.
Sunday:
9:00 a.m. - 9:00 p.m.

Smoking section / Deck seating / Parking lot

Quite unassuming from the outside, the slick interior of Espress Yourself takes you by surprise. A deli case holds sandwich fixings at the small order counter, and a larger soda case artfully displays an array of drinks, including non-alcoholic beer. The shiny black tiled floor and photography on the wall finish the room, but keep walking. The next room is like a den, with couches, plants, and a hardwood floor that continues into the poolroom. Yes—there is a billiards table, and the smoking section, at the back of this coffeehouse, which is beginning to feel more like a resort. Off the back room is the piéce de résistance—the utterly divine deck. A giant oak is the centerpiece for this outdoor setting, which gracefully blends into its residential neighborhood.

SPECIALTIES

Sandwiches, soups, stews, pasta salads

French Meadow Bakery

2610 Lyndale Avenue South

Minneapolis 55408

870-7855

Daily:
6:30 a.m. - 7:00 a.m.

No smoking / Sidewalk seating / Street parking

This high-ceilinged low-lit bakery/deli/coffeehouse offers some great health-conscious choices for every meal of the day. Long cases display a host of tempting meal choices. The words "vegetarian" and "organic" show up on the menu here and there, but decadent desserts abound. Select a newspaper from the sizable rack and relax at one of the handsome tile-topped tables or at the window counter in this long and spacious room. There is an abundance of sidewalk seating during the warm months.

SPECIALTIES

Light breakfast, weekend brunch, hot entrees, salads, sandwiches and award-winning homemade breads

Isles Bun & Coffee Company

1424 West 28th Street

Minneapolis 55408

870-4466

Monday-Friday:
6:30 a.m. - 6:00 p.m.
Saturday-Sunday:
7:00 a.m. - 5:00 p.m.

No smoking / Sidewalk seating / Street parking

Cinnamon buns are baked from scratch in plain view in the sunken kitchen that comprises most of this small shop. Seating is limited to stools at the marble counters along the walls, which are graced with posters from the Minnesota Historical Society. The business is mostly take out, except in the warmer months when there is ample seating out front and plenty of locals taking advantage of it.

SPECIALTIES

Box lunches, sandwiches and savory buns

Java Jack's

818 West 46th Street
Minneapolis 55409
825-2183

*Smoking section / Sidewalk and patio
seating / Street parking*

Monday-Thursday:
6:30 a.m. - 10:00 p.m.
Friday:
6:30 a.m. - 11:00 p.m.
Saturday:
7:30 a.m. - 11:00 p.m.
Sunday:
8 a.m. - 10:00 p.m.

This charming coffeehouse, enormously popular with the local baby boomers, is on the southern edge of Minneapolis in a mostly residential neighborhood. Inside are bright African colors with Jamaican and American artwork, and a cozy windowless nook at one end has its own 1950s decor. At the other end are a few window tables and counter seating. In the main seating area the tables are crowded together during the cold months. During the warm months there is abundant seating on the sidewalk out front and on a deck that winds around to a side patio and then continues into an intimate backyard.

SPECIALTIES

Sandwiches, soups, pasta salad and quiche

Java Z

3617 West 50th Street
Minneapolis 55410
928-0720

*No smoking / Sidewalk seating /
Parking lot*

Monday-Thursday:
6:30 a.m. - 11:00 p.m.
Friday:
6:30 a.m. - Midnight
Saturday:
7:00 a.m. - Midnight
Sunday:
8:00 a.m. - 11:00 p.m.

Each table has fresh cut flowers and the black and white photos of couples kissing set a romantic mood, enhanced by a copper waterfall sculpture and classic music from artists like Sinatra and Bennett. You may choose from several coffees du jour as well as homemade short-breads. There is ample seating at the contemporary little wooden tables and some side bar stools, as well as games and periodicals. Couples can take advantage of the evening "dater's delight": any two espresso drinks and a dessert to share for five dollars.

SPECIALTIES

Breakfast sandwiches, soup, chili and pasta salads

Mojo's Espresso Bar and Deli

3544 Grand Avenue South

Minneapolis 55408

824-2627

*Smoking section / Sidewalk seating /
Street parking*

Monday-Friday:
7:00 a.m. - 9:00 p.m.
Saturday:
9:00 a.m. - 9:00 p.m.
Sunday:
9:00 a.m. - 6:00 p.m

The influence of the neighboring Present Moment Books and Herbs permeates this earthy coffeehouse. Besides the bulletin board jammed with flyers and business cards offering healing classes and services, don't miss Mojo's astrological chart. The hardwood floors, plants in every window, old wooden tables and chairs and nice selection of taped music create a relaxing atmosphere where locals come to chat. Adjoining this room is a cooperative shop which displays local art for sale. Seven coffees of the day are available, as well as Ghirardelli chocolates, Seward Cafe granola and the house special, Mojo's original breakfast burrito.

SPECIALTIES

Breakfast burrito, vegie burgers, sandwiches, salads and
made-to-order burritos

Muddy Waters

2401 Lyndale Avenue South
Minneapolis 55405
872-2232

Monday-Friday:
7:00 a.m. - 11:00 p.m.
Saturday-Sunday:
8:00 a.m. - 11:00 p.m.

Smoking section / Sidewalk seating / Street parking

Notorious for boxed cereals, canned soups, huge Rice Krispies bars and coffee served with an animal cracker, the Muddy Waters menu is surprisingly healthy. A huge "smokeeter" keeps the air breathable for the always sizable crowd, while progressive rock rings through the air. Games, newspapers and outdoor seating are all plentiful. Pink neon lights and the occasional strumming minstrel attract night owls, mostly students and the younger locals.

SPECIALTIES

Light breakfast, sandwiches, bagels, soups

Napoleon's

2447 Hennepin Avenue South
Minneapolis 55405
377-1870

Monday-Friday:
7:00 a.m. - 7:00 p.m.
Saturday-Sunday:
8:00 a.m. - 7:00 p.m.

No smoking / Sidewalk seating / Street parking

Formerly a one-room Jewish bakery with cramped seating, this store has been expanded and remodeled since it was purchased by Napoleon's French bakery. The Jewish influence, however, remains in the kosher selection of pareve (nondairy) breads and desserts and challah bread. Although their goal is eventually to bake exclusively nondairy goods, for now you can enjoy Häagen Dazs bars as well as rich desserts, award-winning breads and several varieties of coffee daily. The new room, with its well-spaced seating, displays artwork for sale and deco wall lamps. Bring a friend and choose from the wooden board games.

SPECIALTIES

Sandwiches and soups

Napoleon's

5009 Penn Avenue South
Minneapolis 55419
928-9722

Monday-Saturday:
7:00 a.m. - 7:00 p.m.
Sunday:
8:00 a.m. - 7:00 p.m.

No smoking / Patio seating / Street parking

This French bakery has a great selection of rich torts, puffs, pies and a rack of day-old breads. Adding more authenticity to the atmosphere is the French music from the radio. This is a single-room, old fashioned bakery setting with patio seating out front in the warm months. Free self-serve coffee refills (take advantage of this nearly-extinct idea) and Häagen Das ice cream bars are available.

SPECIALTIES

Boxed lunches, sandwiches and soups

Nokomis Cup

4956 - 28th Avenue South
Minneapolis 55417
724-5551

No smoking / Sidewalk seating /
Parking slots

Closed Mondays
Tuesday-Friday:
7:00 a.m. - 9:00 p.m.
Saturday-Sunday:
8:00 a.m. - 6:00 p.m.
Winter Hours
Tuesday -Friday:
7:00 a.m. - 5:00 p.m.
Saturday-Sunday:
8:00 a.m. - 6:00 p.m.

Set into a quaint little hamlet, Nokomis cup is spacious and simple. White walls are accented with forest green and plants, and the corner view is of a residential neighborhood. It is a quiet respite from noisy urban shops with its laid back atmosphere, just a block from the east shore of Lake Nokomis. The clientele is mostly families and local residents, giving the shop a neighborhood feel. An extra wide sidewalk, southern exposure and view of the lake provide a nice setting for outdoor seating.

SPECIALTIES

Sandwiches, fruit, yogurt and ice cream

Penny University Coffee House

2221 West 50th Street
Minneapolis 55419
926-3264

No smoking /
Patio seating /
Parking lot

Monday-Thursday:
7:00 a.m. - 10:30 p.m.
Friday: 7:00 a.m. - 11:00 p.m.
Saturday: 8:00 a.m. - 11:00 p.m.
Sunday: 8:30 a.m. - 10:00 p.m.

Winter Hours
Monday: 7:00 a.m.-noon
(rest of day for meetings and
classes–can reserve space)
Tuesday-Thursday:
7:00 a.m. -9:30 p.m.
Friday: 7:00 a.m.-10:30 p.m.
Saturday: 8:00 a.m.-10:30 p.m.
Sunday: 8:00 a.m.-8:00 p.m.

Eighteenth-century English coffeehouses charged a penny to enter and have a cup. Over the years, these gathering places became known as "penny universities." This penny university has a distinctly British menu with Welsh rarebit, homemade potpies, gingerbread, and English curd and marmalade. Order your meal at the counter and sit in one of the two rooms to sip your coffee while waiting for your call. After your meal, head for the "computorium" and finish that writing project on the inhouse rental computer. For an authentic British experience, check out the "Afternoon Cream Tea" on Thursday and Friday, and the "High Tea," a formal affair requiring reservations, on the first Friday of each month.

SPECIALTIES
Breakfast, lunch and dinner

Rendezvou Express

2900 Hennepin Avenue South
Minneapolis 55408
827-1667

Sunday-Thursday:
7:00 a.m. - 10:00 p.m.
Friday-Saturday:
7:00 a.m. - Midnight

Smoking section / Sidewalk seating / Street parking

An old standby for many years, this corner spot offers excellent people watching in the heart of Uptown. There is a fast-food feel to the decor with its steel chairs, veneer benches and formica tables. Here, you can create your own lunch at the sandwich bar and enjoy Greek pastries.

SPECIALTIES

Sandwiches, Greek pies, soups, quiches, salads and
frozen yogurt

Sebastian Joe's

4321 Upton Avenue South
Minneapolis 55410
926-7916

No smoking / Patio seating / Parking lot

Monday-Thursday:
7:00 a.m. - 10:00 p.m.
Friday:
7:00 a.m. - 11:00 p.m.
Saturday:
8:00 a.m. - 11:00 p.m.
Sunday:
8:00 a.m. - 10:00 p.m.

Situated in quaint "downtown" Linden Hills, this popular branch of Sebastian Joe's is a hidden gem of Minneapolis. In the winter months business is mostly take-out, since seating is limited inside. But in warmer weather patrons flock to its lovely leaf-shaded patio and indulge in their premier ice cream. Sebastian Joe's has been creating innovative ice cream flavors for us, as well as many local restaurants, for several years.

SPECIALTIES

Gourmet ice cream

The Red Sky Grill

2300 Hennepin Avenue South
Minneapolis 55405
374-5573

No smoking / Sidewalk seating / Parking lot

This cafeteria setup has a bakery at the far end of the scrubbed tile floor. Benches with snugly arranged tables line its L-shaped length. Recent remodeling provides extra seating in a cozy section up front. Folks come here for the food, especially at lunchtime. Windows all around provide ample reading light while New Age and classical music beckons to baby boomers and up. The Columbian and vanilla-flavored coffees are self-serve with free refills.

SPECIALTIES

Made-to-order sandwiches, soups, chilis and salads

The Upper Crust

2552 Nicollet Avenue
Minneapolis 55404
871-9447

Monday-Friday:
7:00 a.m. - 9:00 p.m.
Saturday-Sunday:
8:00 a.m. - 7:00 p.m.

Smoking section / Sidewalk seating / Street parking

The Upper Crust was one of the first in Minneapolis to offer espresso, and shows no sign of letting up. This urban neighborhood has been growing in ethnicity, with The Black Forest across the street and Greek, Vietnamese and Middle Eastern restaurants nearby. There's plenty of great light pouring through the full-length windows all around. The clientele is mostly local Whittier residents, with people from nearby businesses for lunch. The staff, youthful and radically-dressed, is surprisingly friendly. The bakery products are made on the premises daily. Check out the whole-wheat baguettes for a buck.

SPECIALTIES

Made-to-order sandwiches, soups and pasta salads

Uncommon Grounds

2809 Hennepin Avenue

Minneapolis 55408

872-4811

Sunday-Thursday:
9:00 a.m.-Midnight
Friday-Saturday:
9:00 a.m. - 1:00 a.m.

No smoking / Patio seating / Street parking

Shake the dirt from your boots before stepping into this luxurious living room environment. In this converted South Minneapolis house are four seating areas with rich emerald green banquettes with rose-colored chairs and walls for a plush feel. By day quiet music wafts through, but by night the place comes alive with neighborhood schmoozers. The front yard serves as a lovely patio, surrounded by shrubs and a wrought iron fence.

SPECIALTIES

Sandwiches and soups

Cafe Etc.

Monday-Friday:
10:30 a.m. - 2:30 p.m.
Saturday-Sunday:
Closed

2431 Riverside Avenue

Minneapolis 55454

338-6177

No smoking / Sidewalk seating / Street parking

The bakery and food-prep area take up most of this spacious room, with peripheral seating along the front window and side wall. Everything here is made from scratch with daily choices such as rotini salad with wild rice, French onion soup, key lime pie, German chocolate cake and whole grain bread. Lunch specials and light breakfasts include vegetarian offerings. This clean, white room with a refinished hardwood floor has a harvest theme highlighted by grapevine wreaths. If you've nothing to read, enjoy a bit of free education by watching the cooks. The clientele is mostly from Fairview Hospital and nearby Augsburg College.

SPECIALTIES

Sandwiches, soups and salads

Cafe Noir

1819 Washington Avenue South
Minneapolis 55454
333-1692

Monday-Friday:
7:00 a.m. - 8:00 p.m.
Saturday-Sunday:
8:00 a.m. - 8:00 p.m.

No smoking / Patio seating / Parking lot

This cozy little Seven Corners cafe at the foot of the Tenth Avenue Bridge has a view of law-school students hustling about. The indoor seating is limited, but you can relax on a great cobblestone patio in the warmer months. The parking lot here is a bonus, since parking is always scarce around the University of Minnesota.

SPECIALTIES
Stromboli and Pizette

New Riverside Cafe

329 Cedar Avenue South
Minneapolis 55454
333-4814

*No smoking / Indoor seating only /
Parking lot (validates ¹/₂ time)*

Monday-Thursday:
7:00 a.m. - 11:00 p.m.
Friday:
7:00 a.m. - Midnight
Saturday:
8:00 a.m. - Midnight
Sunday:
9:00 a.m. - 2:00 p.m.

Since 1970 this vegetarian cafe has stood the test of time and shows no sign of tiring. The strength of this place is its dedication to its original cooperative organization, owned by the employees who have always looked as earthy as the food they serve. As legend has it, a priest started the cafe and then "fired" himself and turned the venture into a cooperative. Part of the cooperative arrangement is that as a customer you help yourself to the water and coffee, listen for your name to be hollered when the order is ready, and bus your own dishes. Every meal of the day is remarkable, including the wonderful desserts. At night the cafe becomes an entertainment mecca, with live music that is usually acoustic and folksy.

SPECIALTIES
Full breakfast, lunch and dinner

The Hard Times Cafe

Daily:
5:30 a.m. - 3:00 a.m.

1821 Riverside Avenue
Minneapolis 55454
341-9261

Smoking section / Street parking / Indoor seating only

In keeping with the character of the West Bank, this cafe is co-operatively run as a collective. "We're all managers here." With the original hardwood floors, an old bar, and cigarettes for sale, the atmosphere is heavy with smoke from students and local regulars—a more radical crowd than at the New Riverside Cafe. A bulletin board is jammed with information on current events in the area. The full menu features organically-grown vegetarian food, including many animal-free baked goods.

SPECIALTIES

Full vegetarian menu

Croissants & Sweets

Monday-Friday:
6:00 a.m. - 3:00 p.m.
Closed Weekends

304 Oak Street Southeast
Minneapolis 55414
623-1117

No smoking / Indoor seating only / Street parking

Quiet and off the beaten path from the Washington Avenue bustle, this no-frills shop affords good value on the dollar, and everything is made from scratch. Most of the business is take-out, but there's plenty of room to eat here. The expanded menu includes espresso drinks and vegetarian selections. There are also vending machines for extra beverage choices.

SPECIALTIES

Sandwiches, soups and salads

Espresso Exposé

600 Washington Avenue Southeast
Minneapolis 55414
378-9604

Monday-Friday:
6:30 a.m. - midnight
Saturday-Sunday:
8:00 a.m. - midnight

Smoking section / Indoor seating only / Street parking

Thriving on pure campus energy in the heart of Stadium Village, this large, low-lit room packs in students, instructors and local business people. The low, black ceiling fans keep the air breathable, since half of the space is for smokers. Rock or blues fills the air as well as lots of socializing—not your ideal study atmosphere, though some try. Nonstop street and foot traffic pass by this popular place, directly across from the Radisson Metrodome.

Black Coffee

1701 University Avenue

Minneapolis 55414

331-3437

Monday-Thursday:
10:00 a.m. - 10:00 p.m.
Sunday:
6:00 a.m. - 11:00 p.m.
Closed during the Summer

Smoking section / Indoor seating only / Street parking

Black Coffee is in the basement of the Catholic Student Center and, unlike most coffeehouses, no purchase is required—all are welcome. Come to study or play Ping-Pong, shoot pool or hold forth at the piano. There is a co-op like atmosphere to this non-profit business, which is student-friendly and offers discounts on the food and drinks with a parking stub. Free soup is offered most Wednesdays at noon. Games, periodicals and books are well-stocked. Relax at large and sturdy old wooden tables and chairs, an upholstered living room setting or a wicker nook, and enjoy low music, low lighting and low prices.

SPECIALTIES

Sandwiches and soup

Espresso Royale Caffe

411 14th Avenue Southeast
Minneapolis 55414
623-8127

Monday-Friday:
7:00 a.m. - Midnight
Saturday-Sunday:
8:00 a.m. - Midnight

Smoking section / Sidewalk seating / Street parking

In the heart of Dinkytown, this quintessential coffeehouse, popular with students and professors alike, provides an abundance of small round tables to accommodate the constant crowd. Morning sun brightens the front section of this great room with its mixed decor, ranging from rustic brick to contemporary white to art deco lamps, and a mirrored back wall. Ample reading material is available in the way of periodicals, which are housed in a full-size bookcase. The classical music can barely be heard above the din of conversation.

SPECIALTIES

Sandwiches

Espresso 22

1501 University Avenue Southeast
Minneapolis 55414
378-9555

Monday-Friday:
7:30 a.m. - Midnight
Saturday-Sunday:
9:00 a.m. - Midnight

Smoking permitted / Indoor seating only / Street parking

The second-floor location provides a great overlook of the University campus. This student hangout for the young and restless has games, reference books, a crammed bulletin board, a radical metal sculpture in the corner, intense student art on the walls and Black Sabbath on the stereo—at a reasonable decibel. The big square room is bathed in good reading light from the all-around windows in its Dinkydome confine. The menu is vegetarian and creative, with daily choices like butternut soup with cream and white pepper and couscous salad with raisins and red onion.

SPECIALTIES

Sandwiches, soups and salads

The Purple Onion

326 14th Avenue Southeast
Minneapolis 55414
378-7763

Monday-Friday:
6:30 - Midnight
Saturday-Sunday:
8:00 a.m. - Midnight

Smoking section / Indoor seating only / Street parking

Dim and quiet despite its size, the Purple Onion is bare and beige, but for the fascinating artwork. There is less socializing and more studying. Jazz or blues add to the sultry atmosphere, as does the smoke. The large windows provide the best view of the heart of Dinkytown at this corner. Their pastries are now baked on the premises.

Borders Book Shop and Espresso Bar

Monday-Saturday:
10:00 a.m. - 11:00 p.m.
Sunday:
11:00 a.m. - 8:00 p.m.

1501 South Plymouth Road
Bonaventure Mall
Minnetonka 55305
595-0977

No smoking / Indoor seating only / Parking lot

Enjoy quiet and relaxation while bathing in the full-on western exposure. The coffee bar is on the far side of the bookstore—a veritable oasis. Classical music, jazz or blues flow through the air as browsers wander among the books. Peruse a book at the coffee bar as you sip your cafe au lait, bring a friend and play one of the games, or just gaze out over the Ridge Square Mall and the western sky from the full-length, second-floor windows.

SPECIALTIES

Sandwiches and salads

Caribou Coffee/Book Case

609 East Lake Street
Wayzata 55391
476-1070

*No smoking / Sidewalk seating /
Parking lot*

Monday-Thursday:
6:30 a.m. - 10:00 p.m.
Friday:
6:30 a.m. - 11:00 p.m.
Saturday:
8:00 a.m. - 11:00 p.m.
Sunday:
8:00 a.m. - 10:00 p.m.
Sunday in winter:
8:00 a.m. - 5:00 p.m.

This western locale provides an unobstructed vista from the north shore of Lake Minnetonka. Although the seating is limited in the coffeehouse, you may take your cup and browse in the adjacent bookstore, The Bookcase, which has some seating as well. This Caribou Coffee resembles its sibling shops with its modern design and its popularity with patrons of all ages.

Apotheca Natural Juice Bar

1439 West Lake Street
Minneapolis 55408
824-2474

This hair salon houses a substantial coffee bar. The salon is up-stairs; at street level, apothecary items (soaps, shampoos, etc.) precede the coffee bar in the back. There is a full line of espresso drinks, light breakfasts and sandwiches, with an emphasis on wholesomeness. Unique wrought iron tables on the sidewalk invite an outdoor visit.

Bryant Lake Bowl

810 West Lake Street
Minneapolis 55408
825-3737

Although a mini bowling alley still occupies the back half of this space, Bryant Lake Bowl has been transformed from an arcade that attracted city youth to a beer and wine bar, theater and cafe. By night the place jams, and the bowlers add to the din. But by day it's quiet and relaxing, and there are espresso drinks, coffee and pastries. Big front windows provide plenty of morning light for the two spacious rooms. Full breakfast is served until 1:00 p.m.

Lucia's Wine Bar

1432 West 31st Street
Minneapolis 55408
825-1572

The wine bar, which adjoins the popular cafe, also serves as a coffee bar. There is a full line of espresso drinks in this charming room, with seating both at the bar and at intimate table settings. You will not find the usual pastries here, but killer desserts instead. The wide sidewalk allows for the bar's patio-like seating arrangement during our warm months.

Paulina's

2713 East Lake Street
Minneapolis 55406
724-1718

This bakery has a back kitchen which serves as the preparation headquarters for its restaurants in downtown St. Paul and Northfield. Its French proprieters serve a full line of espresso drinks along with their freshly baked breads and fine French pastries. Their gourmet meals may be ordered as well, but must be called in a few days in advance. If that isn't enough, they also serve ice cream cones.

The Loring Bar & Playhouse

1624 Harmon Place
Minneapolis 55403
332-1617

This bohemian bar serves a hearty dark roast as well as espresso after its 11:30 a.m. opening. Nearby MCC students, artists and others sip coffee under the potted trees in the sun-filled rooms with wonderful old furniture. The sidewalk seating is exceptionally appealing with its flowers and view of Loring Park.

The New French Bar

128 North Fourth Street
Minneapolis 55401
338-3790

Connected to the New French Cafe is its bar on Second Avenue North. Many patronize this spot for its industrial-strength French roast and espresso drinks. This is one of the first places to offer espresso in Minneapolis; many years ago my mother took me there to experience my first café au lait. There is sidewalk seating as well.

Zumbro Cafe

4302 Upton Avenue South
Minneapolis 55410
920-3606

This tiny Linden Hills cafe, known for its gourmet food, also serves espresso drinks and pastries. What's more, there are tables out front in the summer that soak up the best morning sun in town. Bring your shades.

Note: At this writing, a new room is scheduled to open late in 1994 that will serve as a table service restaurant. The original room will focus on coffee drinks and pastries.

St. Paul Coffee Houses

Bad Habit Cafe

418 St. Peter Street

St. Paul 55102

224-8545

Smoking section / Sidewalk seating / Street parking

Monday-Thursday:
7:00 a.m. - 11:00 p.m.
Friday:
7:00 a.m. - 2:00 a.m.
Saturday:
Noon - 2:00 a.m.
Sunday:
Noon - 6:00 p.m.

This alternative environment, an "extension of the living room," was one of the first coffeehouses in St. Paul. "Nun of the Ordinary," announces a coffee card here, where creativity flourishes with the art and jewelry on display, a gothic muralized wall, funky mobiles and a variety of live entertainment most evenings. This tiny spot has the added attraction of an upstairs used-book library in a homier setting. The crowd changes from mostly downtown business folks by day to students by night.

SPECIALTIES

Sandwiches, soups and salads

Francesca's Bakery and Cafe

33 West Seventh Place
St. Paul 55102
227-5775

Monday-Friday:
6:30 a.m. - 6:30 p.m.
Saturday:
7:00 a.m. - 5:00 p.m.
Closed Sunday

*No smoking / Sidewalk seating /
Street parking*

Having established a reputation as a premier bakery, Francesca's has branched out with a wine bar and cafeteria, ultramodern and quite spacious. The espresso and wine bar has its own cozy niche, with bar seating and smaller tables looking out to Landmark Center and the Ordway Theatre. There is something for everyone in this exceptional setting. Don't miss the wonderful desserts and award-winning baked goods.

SPECIALTIES

Sandwiches, soups, pizza & tortas, grilled items, salads
and specialty breads

Kuppernicus Coffee Gallery

308 Prince Street

St. Paul 55101

290-2718

Sunday-Thursday:
7:00 a.m. - 11:00 p.m.
Friday-Saturday:
7:00 a.m. - 1:00 a.m.

Smoking section / Sidewalk seating / Street parking

This epitome of the coffeehouse experience in an old Lower-town warehouse has huge windows, unfinished high ceilings, hardwood floors, massive wooden beams and avant-garde art on the walls. The serene living-room atmosphere provides plenty of elbow room and a chance for private conversations within the well-spaced groupings of couches, armchairs and even a dining room set in the back. Reading light floods in for the diverse crowd of baby boomers, students and artists. The nightly entertainment includes live jazz and blues, classical guitar and films by local artists. Because of its spacious design, this room is rented for private parties, including weddings, and Channel 2 television has often taped here.

Babylon Cafe

267 West Seventh Street

St. Paul 55102

225-9885

Smoking "encouraged" / Sidewalk
and patio seating / Street parking

Monday-Thursday:	5:00 a.m. - 1:00 a.m.
Friday:	5:00 a.m. - 2:00 a.m.
Saturday:	7:00 a.m. - 2:00 a.m.
Sunday:	7:00 a.m. - 1:00 a.m.

Very little is reminiscent of Kuppernicus, of which Babylon's proprietor is a part-owner. This is a handsome New York style bar right down to the black and white tiled floor. Tables line its endless length of adobe brick, and bare branches with strings of lights are slung from above. The bar section is just like your neighborhood pub, and there's a wine bar in the adjoining room. Live entertainment is offered most nights

SPECIALTIES

Sandwiches, salads and stromboli

Blair Caffe

165 Western Avenue

St. Paul 55102

290-9736

*Smoking section / Sidewalk
seating / Parking lot*

Monday-Thursday:
6:00 a.m. - 11:00 p.m.
Friday:
6:00 a.m. - Midnight
Saturday:
7:00 a.m. - Midnight
Sunday:
7:00 a.m. - 10:00 p.m.

Located in the Blair Arcade, this coffeehouse is part of a cultur-
ally diverse corner of St. Paul, along with W. A. Frost, a French
restaurant, a Vietnamese take-out shop and a student art studio. There is no pretense or trendy theme—just a new black-
and-white tiled floor and fresh color on the walls for the mostly
single crowd. The ice cream counter and corner sidewalk tables
make this a fun summer stopover. Part of downtown St. Paul's
skyline and the lovely Basilica down the street can be seen from
these windows. Don't miss the decadant desserts.

SPECIALTIES

Old City Cafe vegetarian entrees, sandwiches, soups,
salads and ice cream

Café con Amoré

917 Grand Avenue

St. Paul 55105

222-6770

Monday-Thursday:
6:30 a.m. - 10:00 p.m.
Friday:
6:30 a.m. - 11:00 p.m.
Saturday:
7:30 a.m. - 11:00 p.m.
Sunday:
8:00 a.m. - 5:00 p.m.

No smoking / Veranda seating / Parking lot

"Coffee with Love" (translated) exudes an Italian flair: art by
Leonardo da Vinci, an historic cartoon mural of Italy, a decor
of grapes and vines and the "Mette e prende Biblioteca," or
put-and-take library, from which you may take a book to return
later or replace with another. The design is beautifully articu-
lated in every detail, from the antique furniture in the front to
the French doors opening to the meeting room in the back.

Caribou Coffee

1055 Grand Avenue
St. Paul 55105
221-0140

Sunday-Thursday:
6:30 a.m. - 10:00 p.m.
Friday-Saturday:
6:30 a.m. - 11:00 p.m.

No smoking / Sidewalk seating / Sidewalk seating

Located in the Oxford Square mall, this shop is a departure from the usual intimate settings in Caribou's chain of coffeehouses. Taking up residence in space that recently housed two shops, the big rectangular room offers an abundance of elbow room as well as seating removed from the commotion of the counter. A lit-up yellow domed inset graces the ceiling, and nearly floor-length windows all around allow a cascade of daylight to flood in. A wholesome blend of families, students and neighborhood residents flock to this store, located next to a Great Harvest Bakery.

Espresso Extra

674 Grand Avenue
St. Paul 55105
225-4127

Monday-Thursday:
7:00 a.m. - 11:00 p.m.
Friday:
7:00 a.m. - Midnight
Saturday:
8:00 a.m. - Midnight
Sunday:
8:00 a.m. - 11:00 p.m.

*Smoking section / Sidewalk seating /
Street parking*

Set off in red, black and white, this large shop has two seating areas: tables on the left and booths on the right—and a lot of space between them for an unobstructed trip to the huge marble counter. The crowd is mostly young and includes students hitting the books, a common sight in many of the St. Paul shops. The special feature is ice-cream cones in a variety of flavors, but don't overlook the dispenser of jawbreakers for the "kids."

Rosie's Coffeehouse

613 Grand Avenue
St. Paul 55102
224-4640

Monday-Thursday:
7:00 a.m. - Midnight
Friday:
7:00 a.m. - 1:00 a.m.
Saturday:
8:00 a.m. - 1:00 a.m.
Sunday:
8:00 a.m. - Midnight

*Smoking section / Sidewalk seating /
Street parking*

Off the beaten Grand Avenue track, this charming coffeehouse has a quiet atmosphere with quaint residential view. Here you'll find classic coffeehouse fare: an inviting case of games and books, folksy or classical music and nicely arranged seating. An Egyptian oasis theme is seen in the mural of the desert pyramid, and lush green plants finish the look. During the evening hours the energy level is bolstered by louder music for nightowl patrons.

SPECIALTIES

Sandwiches, soups, gourmet cakes and ice cream

Midway

Ginkgo Coffeehouse

721 North Snelling Avenue
St. Paul 55104
645-2647

*Smoking section / Patio seating /
Parking lot*

Monday-Thursday:
7:00 a.m. - 10:00 p.m.
Friday:
7:00 a.m. - Midnight
Saturday:
8:00 a.m. - Midnight
Sunday:
8:00 a.m. - 10:00 p.m.

Here's a classic coffeehouse with old hardwood floors, a high ceiling, ample space for monthly art exhibits, a mini gift shop that features greeting cards, and a hodgepodge of miniature rubber animals for sale by the front door. The Thursday night concerts, with a cover charge, are reminiscent of the Cedar Cultural Center and the New Folk Collective. Wednesday is open-stage night. People of all ages, students and neighborhood residents appreciate the specialty coffee drinks, including "the best cappucino in town."

SPECIALTIES

Sandwiches, soups, baked potatoes with toppings, Old City Cafe vegetarian items and ice cream in the summer

Susan's Coffeehouse & Deli

2399 University Avenue

St. Paul 55114

644-7906

Monday-Friday:
7:00 a.m. - 7:00 p.m.
Saturday:
9:00 a.m. - 5:00 p.m.
Closed Sunday

No smoking / Sidewalk seating / Street parking

This is a spacious setting in an old building just east of Highway 280, with high ceilings and hardwood floors. Ample seating and sultry jazz invite a leisurely stay amid a more sophisticated crowd in this earthy setting. This full-fledged deli offers plenty of choices—orange curry lentil salad was the special one Monday. There are imported crackers, chips, chocolate-covered espresso beans, candy and novelty books for sale. Otherwise, relax with one of the used books or periodicals up front.

SPECIALTIES

Light breakfast, full lunch and dinner

The Coffee Grounds

1579 Hamline Avenue
Falcon Heights 55108
644-9959

Monday-Thursday:
6:45 a.m. - 9:00 p.m.
Friday-Saturday:
7:00 a.m. - 11:00 p.m.
Sunday:
8:00 a.m. - 9:00 p.m.

No smoking / Outdoor seating / Parking lot

Step down into this unique coffeehouse with antique wooden furniture. Catering to neighborhood baby boomers, Coffee Grounds dubs itself "family friendly." There are games and books for both children and adults, as well as the Interstellar Propeller Hat, their novelty gift item. A kids club features monthly educational presentations. By day this place attracts a mix of nearby business folks, retired people and moms taking a break while the kids are in school. Soothing classical or New Age music fills the air. By night the music is more diverse and the place attracts dating and married couples. Live entertainment is featured on weekends.

SPECIALTIES

Sandwiches, soup and ice cream

Lori's Coffee House

Monday-Friday:
7:00 a.m. - 11:00 p.m.
Saturday-Sunday:
9:00 a.m. - 11:00 p.m.

1441 North Cleveland
St. Paul 55108
647-0833

No smoking / Outdoor seating /
Street parking

This handsome midsize shop has brick accents, bright red seats and a painted green ceiling. The view is a section of the beautiful St. Paul Campus of the University of Minnesota. A grand old residential neighborhood lies behind this small strip of shops that includes a photocopy service, hair salon and food mart. Soft music, games, periodicals and reference books encourage a stay. A photo exhibit shared the walls with potato prints one month, as well as kids' crayon drawings. Track lighting and the blue neon coffee cup finish the sharp look.

SPECIALTIES

Soup, basket of fruit, bread and cheese

A Fine Grind

2038 Marshall Avenue

St. Paul 55104

641-0230

Monday-Friday:
6:00 a.m. - Midnight
Saturday-Sunday:
7:30 a.m. - Midnight

Smoking allowed / Sidewalk seating / Street parking

A large store with ample seating and a wide variety of music, the motive here is to offer students a place to throw down their books and stay awhile. Its late-night hours accommodate studiers from nearby high schools and colleges, while daytime hours provide mostly take-out business. The decor is a Spanish motif of the Granada region, with lots of brick and stonework along the walls and bar. In the warm months there is outdoor seating that extends into the painted alley.

SPECIALTIES

Middle-Eastern selections, Italian deli sandwiches on focaccia, pocket-pizza sandwiches, soup du jour and pasta salad

Brewberry's

475 Fairview Avenue South
St. Paul 55105
699-1117

*No smoking / Outdoor seating /
Parking lot*

Monday-Thursday:
6:30 a.m.-10:00 p.m.
Friday:
6:30 a.m.-11:00 p.m.
Saturday:
7:30 a.m.-11:00 p.m.
Sunday:
7:30 a.m.-6:00 p.m.

Originally a gas station, the exterior of this coffeehouse displays wildflowers where pumps were and the overhead extension now serves as shelter for outdoor patrons. The interior is simply charming, with flowers everywhere: on tabletops, in wreaths, baskets and counter vases—even a flowered tapestry fabric on the chairs. Two rooms make up the L-shaped seating area, which accommodates plenty of visitors and provides an abundance of light from the tall windows. Mostly neighborhood women and students flock to this residential location adjacent to the Mississippi Market. The *Pioneer Press* has its own rack inside, and a collection of games are available for use as well.

SPECIALTIES
Salads and sandwiches

Cuppa Joe

1662 Grand Avenue
St. Paul 55105
699-9271

Monday-Friday:
6:00 a.m. - 10:00 p.m.
Saturday:
8:00 a.m. - 10:00 p.m.
Sunday:
8:00 a.m. - 8:00 p.m.

Smoking permitted / Sidewalk seating / Street parking

A lively and attractive coffeehouse, from the hardwood floors to the earth-tone colors, Cuppa Joe has three sections: a front overlooking Grand Avenue, a middle with tables and benches along the wall opposite the serving counter, and a back area for smokers. Every seat has just enough light to read but not enough to highlight blemishes. The crowd seems to be at home in this earthy setting. The sizable bulletin board is kept current and uncluttered. A green painted case houses some interesting hardcovers and another offers self-serve bulk beans.

SPECIALTIES

Sandwiches, soup, Middle Eastern appetizers, baguettes and fruit

Dunn Bros. Coffee

1569 Grand Avenue

St. Paul 55105

698-0618

Monday-Thursday:
6:30 a.m.-11:00 p.m.
Friday:
6:30 a.m.-Midnight
Saturday-Sunday:
7:30 a.m.-Midnight

Smoking section / Sidewalk and patio seating / Parking lot

This is such a popular coffeehouse that patrons have occasion to share tables in order to stay. There are two rooms and the roaster in the back, with all its fanfare. Some folks cluster into the small front section by the counter while most pile into the adjoining room. The stage offers a bit more seating until it provides entertainment in the evening. The modest decor is light green walls, dark green benches and some large plants, along with quite an assortment of Dunn Bros. Coffee souvenirs. This is where it's at for a diverse crowd.

Gijo's Coffee Bar

1811 Selby Avenue
St. Paul 55104
647-1265

No smoking / Sidewalk seating / Street parking

Nestled amid antique shops in a residential neighborhood, this down-home, no-frills coffeehouse attracts mostly locals and some students. The baked goods are made from scratch on the premises, and the specialty is mouth-watering scones of varying flavors. There is a Scandinavian feel to the simple decor with its imported "tee" and a Danish-looking rack stuffed with periodicals. The shelf of games for adults and kids includes crayons, which explains the drawings covering the side of the refrigerator.

SPECIALTIES

Sandwiches, soups, including vegetarian, salads,
and chips and salsa

Table of Contents

1648 Grand Avenue

St. Paul 55105

699-6595

Monday-Thursday:
9:00 a.m. - 9:30 p.m.
Friday-Saturday:
9:00 a.m. - 11:00 p.m.
Sunday:
10:00 a.m. - 9:00 p.m.

No smoking / Patio seating / Parking lot

Though a full-fledged restaurant with a beer and wine bar, Table of Contents functions as a coffeehouse before and after the dinner hour. Its lobby, shared with The Hungry Mind Bookstore, is full of every conceivable piece of free literature to be had in St. Paul. Inside the graceful design is modern yet unpretentious, industrial yet soft. Tables and chairs are black matte and a wall is adorned with black art-deco lamps. Exposed ducts are suspended from the open, unconfined ceiling, which has a great skylight. The counter is light hardwood with hanging lamps above. A larger room accommodates the coffeehouse overflow as well as the restaurant crowd. Music is jazzy and low to suit the sophisticated clientele.

SPECIALTIES

Light breakfast, gourmet lunches and dinners,
and Sunday brunch

Napoleon's

1806 St. Clair Avenue

St. Paul 55105

690-0178

Monday-Friday:
6:30 a.m. - 7:00 p.m.
Saturday:
7:00 a.m. - 6:00 p.m.
Sunday:
7:00 a.m. - 4:00 p.m.

No smoking / Sidewalk seating / Street parking

This French bakery, one of four in the Twin Cities, offers gorgeous European pastry, and everything is made from scratch, including the soups. Off the bakery are two rooms with racks of local publications and fresh flowers on each table. The back room has French-influenced art and a lovely antique buffet. There is a Häagen Dazs case and fresh pizza to go, as well as a day-old rack of baked goods to take advantage of.

SPECIALTIES

Box lunches, sandwiches and soup

102 Macalester-Groveland

Trotter's Country Bakery

232 North Cleveland Avenue

St. Paul 55104

645-8950

Tuesday-Friday:
7:00 a.m. - 7:00 p.m.
Saturday:
7:00 a.m. - 4:00 p.m.
Closed Sunday

No smoking / Sidewalk seating /
Street parking

Soft music and well-tended plants enhance this quaint setting of two small rooms with polished hardwood floors and handsome furniture. In one room lovely antique-looking cases display intriguing pastries such as "chocolate chaos cupcakes." Breads figure prominently, with varieties such as oat sunflower millet and whole-wheat herb. The other room, like a little deli, has a small refrigerated display of salads, fruits and daily specials, like tabouli salad. The extensive desserts are offered in catered quantities as well.

SPECIALTIES

Hot entrees, boxed lunches, sandwiches, soups
and hearty salads

The Roastery

769 Cleveland Avenue
St. Paul 55116
699-5448

Monday-Thursday:
6:30 a.m. - 9:00 p.m.
Friday-Saturday:
6:30 a.m. - 10:00 p.m.
Sunday:
8:00 a.m. - 5:00 p.m.

*No smoking / Sidewalk seating / Street
parking*

As you enter this spacious and family-friendly coffeehouse, you will encounter burlap bags filled with beans from the latest tasting session. The red roaster beams like a well-polished fire engine. Beans are roasted daily and sold within three days (to maintain freshness) or are then donated to food shelves. Friendly servers can offer expert advice while you sample the daily brews. A children's play area in the back encourages young moms to meet here for fellowship. There's mellow music, fresh flowers on each table and a variety of accessories for sale.

Caribou Coffee

2138 Ford Parkway

St. Paul 55116

690-9934

Sunday-Thursday:
6:30 a.m. - 10:00 p.m.
Friday-Saturday:
6:30 a.m. - 11:00 p.m.

No smoking / Sidewalk seating / Parking lot

Highland Park has its second coffeehouse, this one located in the Highland Village mall. Like its 44th and France store, this small shop has access to an adjoining Bruegger's Bagels. Its interior is Jetson green with the slung ceiling piece that Caribou is fond of. The streamlined bar overlooks Bruegger's through a giant window, and there are half a dozen tables up front as well. Check out the rich desserts.

SPECIALTIES

Light breakfast, sandwiches, stuffed Italian pastry and soups

GLOSSARY OF TERMS

CAFÉ AMERICANO

Filtered hot water added to a shot of espresso (full-flavored and satisfying yet mild as brewed coffee)

CAFÉ AU LAIT

The real thing is made with equal parts drip-brewed French roast coffee and heated milk poured simultaneously into a café au lait bowl, but many coffeehouses make it with espresso and steamed milk.

CAFÉ BREVE

A creamy drink of espresso and steamed half-and-half

CAFÉ LATTE

A shot of espresso in a tall glass filled with steamed milk and topped with little or no foam

CAFÉ MIEL

Swirls of honey coat the cup as steamed milk and espresso are poured in, topped with whipped cream.

CAFÉ MOCHA

Espresso mixed with steamed milk and chocolate syrup and usually topped with whipped cream sprinkled with cocoa powder

CAFÉ RISTRETTO

"Restricted" espresso uses only 1 ounce of water and the same amount of coffee grounds to make the strongest and most concentrated of espressos.

Its name is derived from the foamy cap on the drink which resembles the cowl, or cappuccino, worn by Capuchin friars. A "wet" cappuccino is made by using approximately ⅓ espresso, ⅓ hot steamed milk and ⅓ foamed milk. A "dry" cappuccino is a shot of espresso with the remainder of the cup filled with foam.

ELIXIR

A thick coating of sweetened condensed milk that clings to the walls of the cup as espresso is poured in

ESPRESSO

One shot (about 1 ounces) of espresso served in a 2½ ounce cup

ESPRESSO MACCHIATO

An espresso "marked" with a dollop of milk foam (pronounced mock-e-ah-toe)

FLAVORED SYRUPS

Originating in Italy, these caffeine free nonalcoholic syrups come in dozens of flavors. The fruit flavors are best in soda water (Italian soda) or iced drinks, and the nut, spice and richer flavors are more suited to hot coffee drinks.

ICED ESPRESSO

One shot of espresso and one shot of milk poured over ice

LATTE MACCHIATO

A cup of steamed milk "marked" with a spot of espresso. The steamed milk is added first, then topped with foam, and the espresso is added last by pouring it through the foam, which leaves the "mark."

STEAMER

Steamed milk with a flavored syrup. Almond, vanilla and hazel-nut are popular.

Excerpts taken from Espresso *by Petzke and Slavin and* Cappuc-cino/Espresso: The Book of Beverages *by Christie and Thomas Katona.*

ESPRESSO IS . . .

The Coffee: A blend of specifically selected varietal coffees that are roasted together to a very dark and oily level. The resulting coffee has an almost nutty sweetness.

The Roast: As described above, when you roast coffee to a dark and oily level, that "darkness" is called an "espresso roast." Other levels of roasting are called "French," "Italian," etc.

The Drink: That hot, very small (2.5 oz), very rich, very intense drink is called "an espresso."

The Machine: A properly made espresso can only be made in an espresso machine that is capable of pushing hot water and steam through the finely ground espresso coffee.

The Grind: When you look at a commercial coffee grinder, there is a setting on the machine that says "espresso." Any coffee can be ground to an "espresso grind."

Therefore, espresso is the name for the coffee, the roasting level, the actual drink, the machine used to make the drink and the fineness of the grind.

Reprinted from "What You Should Know Before You Buy," *with permission from Joe Anderson of Kafté.*

ABOUT THE AUTHOR

A Minneapolis native, Ruth Rasmussen has long enjoyed the coffeehouse atmosphere, finding it conducive to writing and relaxing. In 1989, while studying English at UCLA in Los Angeles, she wrote restaurant critiques for a Los Angeles newspaper and went on to freelance for a public-relations agency that specialized in the restaurant business. After returning to Minneapolis she worked as a travel magazine photo editor, newsletter editor, and writer for a southwest Minneapolis newspaper. By the summer of 1993, the coffeehouse boom was underway in the Twin Cities—it was becoming hard to keep track of them all. One day a friend suggested a guidebook . . .